MW01286898

LETTERS TO MY DAUGHTER

By

K.T.Burkeen

Content

Dedication

This book is dedicated to my oldest daughter Kate, and all the parents that has ever lost a child are a child that has lost a parent.

About the Author

While growing up in a small town with a population of 500, K.T., known as Katie, was adopted by her grandparents at the age of one. She lived most of her life in Bedias, TX and was married once and divorced. She is also a mother of two beautiful daughters and a tire designer. She has worked at her local church doing management work since 2017. During her free time, she enjoys watching movies, writing, reading, traveling, and just spending time with family and friends.

Chapter 1

Even now, as I sit here thinking back on that awful day in 2013, I am still able to recall the whirlwind of emotions that went over me. My heart thumped so hard I thought it would explode out of my chest; every beat a reflection of the agony that engulfed me. Unchecked, tears ran down my cheeks, mixing with the searing anguish engraved into my face to leave behind salty tracks.

Looking back on those early days and realizing how young I was when I became your mother is an incredible experience. I was a teenager managing my ups and downs while also taking care of a newborn. But even in the midst of difficulties, you were my tiny bundle of joy—the light in my dark and the love of my life.

Then, I experienced a heartbreaking moment as I saw you vanish. It seemed as though your father was taking you from me, gradually eroding your hold on me. This was the most heartbreaking experience of my life; it was like having a piece of my heart ripped out.

When I met your dad in 2009, that's when we began our journey together. I was a young teenager living with my grandparents in a little rural village, taking care of them with love. Unlike the busy cities you see in movies, our town was calm and peaceful, with not too many people about and not too much noise. Its own enchantment made it stand out from other places. In retrospect, I see that I started a new chapter in my life when I met your dad.

I was just 14 when I saw him for the first time. It's been said that love is blind to color, and I believe this to be true. I didn't see anything but his charming smile and friendly ways. I couldn't help but wonder how someone could be so captivating.

I saw him fishing with his family on the lake one day. I was drawn to him like a magnet because of something about him. Despite my nervousness and lack of confidence, I couldn't help but feel the want to approach him and have a conversation.

I was excited and nervous at the same time as I drew near. How would he perceive me? Does he think I'm even here? But in spite of my reservations, I moved forward because I was determined to talk to this fascinating man.

When I go back, I see how innocent I was. Despite my lack of knowledge about relationships or love, I was eager to take the risk and explore where this accidental meeting would take me.

There were benefits to living by the lake, but there were also drawbacks. Although it appeared like destiny was putting us together, I was forced to wish that things had turned out differently and that our paths had never met.

I was drawn to him, though, and I couldn't shake that feeling. His presence had a certain quality that gave me a sense of aliveness and opened my eyes to the universe. So, ready to go out on a journey that would alter my life irreversibly, I took a deep breath and approached him with a blend of excitement and anxiety.

I grabbed up the guts to approach him, and we started up a conversation. He seemed sociable and extroverted, which put me at ease. I said hello, told him how cute I thought he was, and congratulated him. But at first, he appeared a little hesitant, maybe because I looked so much younger. He was fifteen years older than me, and when I disclosed my age, it became clear how old we were.

I couldn't help but wonder whether my grandparents knew about our chat and how they would react. Given the gap in our ages, I knew they wouldn't be in favor of our relationship. We kept talking and got to know one another better in spite of this worry.

As we got to know one another better, his charisma and character drew me in. When I was with him, I felt as though I was the only person in the world. I was young and inexperienced, yet I couldn't help but connect deeply with him.

We are somewhat different in age, so I was concerned about what other people would think of our relationship. Were they gonna criticize us for our relationship? Would they notice our differences simply or would they recognize the connection we had?

I couldn't shake the sentiments I had for him in spite of these doubts. Above all, he made me happy. He also made me giggle and felt special. Isn't happiness what really counts in the end?

It was a custom for my grandfather and I to go fishing at the lake. I couldn't help but look around every time we went in the hopes of seeing your dad. In retrospect, I wish I had given my grandfather's worries more thought. That day, he caught us talking and told me to stay away from that older man. But, my obstinate self was overcome by your dad's charm, oh boy.

Adolescence may be challenging, especially if you start feeling something for someone you know isn't right. It seems as though your emotions and mind are always at odds with one another. Despite your best efforts to listen to logic, those emotions are unavoidable. I've undoubtedly absorbed that lesson the hard way, my dear.

The way love works is funny, isn't it? You can accomplish things that you never would have imagined. Like taking unimaginable risks or disobeying the advice of people who love you. However, everything seems worthwhile at the time, doesn't it? It feels like nothing else in the world matters when you experience that emotional rush and butterflies in your stomach.

I see now how ignorant I was. When I was a little child, I was engulfed in the storm of feelings that accompany a first love. I was unable to go past the obvious and consider the possible repercussions of my conduct. Regardless of what others might think or say, all I knew was that I wanted to be close to your dad.

Thus, my love, if I could give you one bit of advice, it would be to pay attention to the people who are close to you. Their goals are good, even though they might not always be correct. And sometimes it helps to stand back and give things some serious thought when it comes to matters of the heart. You'll thank yourself in the end, I promise.

Weeks passed, but I still couldn't help but be pulled to the lake in the hopes of seeing him. Making the daily trip down there to check if he was around became something of a ritual. In retrospect, I see how much of an influence he had on me—how his presence dominated my thoughts and controlled my behavior.

No matter how hard I tried, I was unable to get him out of my head. He seemed to have cast a spell on me, permeating every aspect of my existence. It began to impact me in unexpected ways. He became the center of my universe, and my entire way of life centered around him. I lost all interest in other things and was unable to enjoy the things I had previously enjoyed. I felt as though I was unable to see above the cloud of my own emotions, as though I were living in a fog.

I can see now how emotionally misguided and ignorant I was. As a teenager, I was attempting to make sense of this strange connection that had taken over my life while coping with emotions I didn't understand. But at that time, all I could think about was him, and how much I wanted to be with him.

I wish I could go back in time and tell her, when she was younger, that her sentiments were not love at all but infatuation. True love needs time to bloom and develop into something meaningful and long-lasting. But at the moment, I was too immersed in the fiction to notice the truth.

I followed him around every day, hoping that one day he might feel the same way about me. It was a futile endeavor, I recognize now, but at the time it appeared to be all that mattered. I was unaware that there was still to be learned the most crucial lesson of all.

I used to remember sitting in my bedroom and watching the stars glitter in the night sky through the window. I did this for countless evenings, counting every glistening star in the sky and wishing upon each one as it sped through the night. I dreamed of a future with him, the guy who had won my heart, and my heart was filled to the brim with hope and longing.

I imagined myself living a contented life with him by my side, starting a family together. Oh, how I loved those dreams, how I held them near and dear to my heart like precious stones. Time seemed to pass slowly while I waited for him to return, making each day feel endless.

I used to run out of the house every morning in the hopes of seeing him by the lake, where he and his family would frequently go fishing. I clung resolutely to the schedule, which became into a daily habit for me. And then, one day, as I stood by the water's edge, my heart skipped a beat as I saw a familiar brown truck approaching.

My heart rate shot up as he pulled up next to me, and I experienced mixed emotions of happiness and anxiety. I blushed as he murmured, "Hello again," and smiled sweetly at me. "Hiiiiii," gasping for air, I stammered, uneasy in his presence.

He then shocked me by asking to take a trip into town, saying he had some errands to run and would be right back. I had conflicting ideas racing through my head and didn't know what to do. I wanted, on the one hand, to be with him more, to take advantage of this chance to get close to the man who was enslaving my heart. However, I was hesitant since I knew that might not be the best choice.

My grandfather's voice called my name from a distance, interrupting my daydream before I could reply. I knew I had to decline his offer and return home, and I felt a tinge of regret. Before we left, though, he asked for my phone number, which I kindly provided in the hopes that we would cross paths again soon.

I experienced a range of emotions as I watched him drive out, including excitement, nervousness, and a small amount of remorse for the opportunity wasted. Still, I harbored a secret hope that our paths would ultimately cross again and that things would come together to bring us back together. And with that in mind, I turned and headed back home, bringing the promise of more to come along with the memory of our brief meeting.

I noticed that as our connection grew, I became more and more dependent on him. I was so desperate to talk to him, even if it was just over the phone, that I called him nonstop. I wanted nothing more than to feel and hear his voice. However, in order to conceal our discussions from my watchful grandparents, I had to be discreet while using our outdated landline phone, taking care not to be discovered.

Even though it was risky, our talks—which often lasted for hours on end—became the highlight of my days. We discussed everything and anything, but mostly we planned how to sneak about and meet up with each other when he came back to town. He was frequently on the road between Texas and Louisiana because he was a manager for an outdoor retailer. He and his family used to rent a cabin by the lake where I lived every time he came to visit.

My life's greatest moments were spent laughing, having new experiences, and spending snatched minutes with him during those weekends. I relished every moment we shared, taking in the beauty of the outdoors and the coziness of his companionship. But as time went on, I noticed a pattern: he would frequently be missing, going for extended periods of time without saying anything to me or his own family.

I initially dismissed it as being part of his employment, thinking that his frequent travels were just a perk. However, I couldn't get rid of the uneasy feeling that crept up on me whenever he was gone. I yearned to get nearer to him, to close the distance that separated us.

So I started going to the lake on daily basis in the hopes of seeing him and relishing the brief minutes we had together. However, there were occasions when he failed to appear at all, which baffled me and made me feel let down. It was during those times when I started to wonder if his heart was really as engaged in us as mine was, and I started to doubt the genuine nature of our connection.

I held onto the notion that our love would remain and that our link would be strong enough to overcome the difficulties that lay ahead, even in the face of uncertainty. So I just waited and watched, hoping and praying that one day he would come back to me, eager to start where we left off and write the next chapter in our shared tale.

He was everything to me, in my opinion. He was like the sun in my sky, beaming brightly and chasing away any uncertainty or anxiety-inducing shadows. I was of the firm notion that he was incapable of doing anything wrong. I had no idea that I was going to go off on a quest of knowledge that would completely alter the way I saw the complexity of love.

I jumped out of bed with a sense of exhilaration in my veins as the early sun peaked through my window. I quickly put on my clothes, paying close attention to how I brushed my hair and applied my makeup. I dreamed of the day we would finally be together again, on the lake where our love originally flowered, with every brushstroke.

I rushed joyfully to the door, ready to start the day and be with my beloved again. But before I could step outside, my sister's voice stopped me in my tracks. "Where are you off to so early?" she inquired, her curiosity piqued by my sudden departure. Without missing a beat, I replied, "Just heading to the lake for some fresh air."

I was unable to lie to my family members, especially not to my sister, who always appeared to be able to tell when I was lying. She was fully aware that I was heading to see the one who possessed my heart. She gave me a knowing smile and waved me away, acknowledging in silence the attraction that kept drawing me to him.

The breathtaking beauty of the sunrise, which painted the sky in shades of pink and orange, as I made my way towards the lake, left me speechless. I was reminded of the small pleasures that were waiting for me near the water's edge by this amazing sight. My exhilaration, fed by the hope of seeing him again, increased with every step.

I was surrounded by a bustling crowd of people by the lake, all of them lost in their own little worlds. I scanned the crowd, trying to find a familiar face amid the many new ones, and I prayed he would be there to embrace me. However, I was horrified to see that he had vanished from sight as I turned to look around.

I searched every inch of lake in the hopes of spotting him among the throng. But no matter how hard I looked, I couldn't find him. Rather, I was encircled by his relatives, all of whom were quite similar to him. It was as though he had abandoned fragments of himself all over the lake, serving as a constant reminder of the love that united them.

I was disappointed to see him go and made the decision to head back home, accepting that he would not be waiting for me. As I was about to walk away, I heard a welcome voice from behind me. When I glanced around, I saw another man standing there with a sun-warm smile. "Hello," I replied, returning his greeting with a shy smile of my own. He introduced himself, and we struck up a conversation, our words flowing easily between us. Before I knew it, we were exchanging numbers, the promise of a new connection blooming between us.

The day had taken an unexpected turn, leaving me feeling bewildered by the whirlwind of emotions swirling inside me. One moment, I had set out in search of your dad, my heart filled with hope and anticipation. And now, here I was, standing face to face with his cousin, a stranger who somehow felt familiar.

I had the impression that there was something unique about him while we spoke, something that pulled me to him in a manner that I couldn't quite put my finger on. Even with all of the confusion and doubt in my thoughts, I could not help but be drawn to him and be enthralled with his presence.

Amidst the serene beauty of the lake, I sensed a spark of something new at that precise moment— something that hinted to possibilities that were still ahead. I couldn't help but wonder what was ahead for us as I left, keeping his number tucked firmly in my pocket.

The ache in my heart persisted as I wiped away my tears, feeling the weight of sadness settling over me like a heavy blanket. With each step homeward, the burden of hurt clung to me, etching lines of sorrow upon my face.

I went to my room, which felt like a refuge, and fell onto my bed to take comfort in being alone myself. I prayed silently to the sky above, asking to hear your father's voice again, even if it was just for a brief while, in the quiet solitude.

I sighed in frustration, tossed away his cousin's number, the object of my festering resentment, and got up, resolved to get in touch with him again. I shook hands and gripped the house phone, dialing his number, the digits a lifeline to the one person who could calm my anxious spirit.

To my astonishment, he answered on the first ring, his voice a balm to my fractured spirit. "Hello," he said, the sound of his greeting sending a shiver down my spine. Unable to contain my emotions, I was swept away by a flood of tears, my voice choked with longing as I whispered his name.

"Katie, is that you?" With a soft lilt in his voice, he asked, clearly showing worry. I breathed a weak breath and gave him my full identify, my heart torn open. I was at a loss for words at that point because my need was too intense to put into words.

I spilled my heart to him, admitting my want for his presence, my desperation evident with each shaky confession, and he listened, a mute witness to my suffering. Even though there was a physical distance between us, I felt a spark of optimism and a connection throughout that brief discussion.

"I'm sorry," he said, his voice tinged with remorse, "I've been out of town. But I should have at least called you." His words, though belated, carried a sincerity that resonated with me.

"Yes," I replied softly, "it would have been nice to hear your voice." The absence of his calls had left a void in my days, a silence that echoed with longing.

"I thought you moved on from me already," I confessed, my words catching in my throat, choked with emotion. The fear of abandonment gnawed at me, threatening to engulf me in its suffocating embrace.

With a reassuring tone, he dispelled my doubts. "I wouldn't move on without you," he declared, his words a beacon of hope in the darkness of uncertainty. "I really like you." His admission sent a flutter of warmth through my heart, a confirmation of the bond that bound us together.

Those words, spoken with such earnestness, etched themselves into my memory, a refrain that echoed within me like a cherished melody. In the quiet moments of solitude, they served as a reminder of the connection we shared, a thread that tethered us across the miles.

And so, as we lingered on the line, reluctant to part ways, he made a promise to return to me. "I'll be back down within a few weeks to see you," he assured me, his commitment unwavering.

"Okay," I replied, my voice filled with a mixture of hope and apprehension. "I hope you are right." Though doubts lingered in the recesses of my mind, I chose to hold onto his words, clinging to the promise of his imminent return.

I didn't know how to bring it up to him. I had met one of his cousins, and he even gave me his number. But I couldn't bring myself to reach out to him. My feelings for your dad were too strong, too deep. I just couldn't imagine talking to another man, not when my heart belonged to your dad.

So, instead of reaching out to his cousin, I simply told him that I would be waiting for your dad's call when he got back to the lake. I promised to come down to see him as soon as he reached out. I couldn't bear the thought of missing even a moment with him.

Your dad, he wasn't like other guys. He never took it easy on me, even though I was just a girl at the time. But that's what drew me to him. He challenged me, pushed me to be better. And despite the ups and downs, I knew deep down that he was the one I wanted to give my heart to.

I prayed to God every day that he would be the one I could fully commit myself to. And my heart would race with anticipation each time I heard his voice on the other end. I was reminded that love was worth fighting for by what seemed to be a glimmer of hope peeking through the clouds.

I continued my day after that, spending time with my family. We laughed and enjoyed ourselves while

21

playing a game of bingo together. My mood would always improve when I was among them.

Having a phone conversation with your dad usually makes me feel better. It gave me the impression that everything would be simpler and that I could handle anything. Hearing his voice was like earning a million dollars every time.

Chapter 2

T ime passed slowly, and every day felt like it would never end as I waited impatiently for any updates on your dad's return. Without being able to look away, I was waiting for the phone to ring so I could hear his voice once more. With him at my side, I envisioned a lifetime of love and bliss, conjuring up vivid pictures of an idealized past.

Weeks and maybe even months might pass without receiving a single call. Even yet, I held onto the recollections of our times together and treasured them in the depths of my heart, despite the protracted pauses. He did follow through on his commitment to return, but the two weeks he had previously suggested were simply too long to wait. It felt more like an eternity.

When he did come back, it was one of those nights that I would never forget—like a scene from a romance film. I remember the precise moment he beckoned me outside, his voice comforting and gentle as he urged me to go outside into the beautiful night and stroll in the direction of the lake. My pulse was racing with expectation as I quickly put on my shoes and ran out the door, feeling a mixture of confusion and excitement.

My breath was taken away by what I saw as I arrived at the lake. There he stood, glowing softly in the moonlight near the edge of the river. Anxiety and intense feeling combined to propel my legs as I moved in his direction. I ran into him at last and threw myself in his arms, tears pouring down my cheeks. He promised that he would never let me go again, and in that instant, all the need and anxiety vanished.

It was a magical night, a time of unadulterated happiness that appeared to stop time itself. And there, in his arms, beneath the moonlit sky, with the prospect of an unending future ahead of us, I felt deep down that this was where I belonged. We stood there, encircled by each other's embrace.

That night became the most amazing night ever for me. I was with the man I was starting to fall in love with. We walked together, holding hands, as we laughed and smiled a lot. We had the impression of being the only two persons in the world. We went to his parents' lakeside cabin as the night became late. We had the place to ourselves because they weren't there. Being there with him seemed like something really special.

Lying in your father's arms for the first time was like a dream come true. His embrace made me feel warm and safe. I remember resting my head on his chest, listening to the rhythm of his heartbeat. It was a comforting sound, like a lullaby. I felt so peaceful and content in that moment. We started kissing, and soon, it led to us making love. It was my first time experiencing such intimacy with someone.

At first, I was nervous and unsure, but your dad was gentle and patient with me. He took things slowly, making sure I felt comfortable every step of the way.

I was both nervous and excited at the same time as we shared that moment. But I felt I was in good hands with your dad by my side. I had never felt alive until I sensed his passion and tenderness. I was happy to enjoy the lovely event with someone who was as considerate as he was.

Being with your dad that night was magical. It was like time stood still, and we were in our own little world. We talked for hours, sharing our hopes and dreams. We laughed at silly jokes and whispered secrets to each other. It was a night I would never forget.

As the hours passed, our bond grew stronger. It felt like we had known each other forever. Every touch, every smile, felt so natural and right. I knew then that I was falling deeply in love with him. And being in his arms, surrounded by the quiet beauty of the lake, made everything feel perfect.

I knew that love would hurt, but I also knew that it could heal, and making love to him was very healing and satisfying.

The night grew longer when we were so close together and comfortable. I was becoming a woman now. When we initially met, I was fifteen years old, but when we made love, I was sixteen. 2010: That evening, I told your dad that I wanted to marry him and have his kids. He grinned and looked up at me before giving me a kiss and telling me that one day you will be. When morning finally arrived, I had to return home before my grandparents discovered that I was gone. So I got dressed and told him I had to leave now. But please come back to me. Of course I will, he said. Then, I walked out to the end of my house's driveway. He kissed me, and then walked away. As I was walking inside, I turned back around and yelled out, "I LOVE YOU," with tears coming down my face.

I realized I was in love when I heard murmured declarations of love in the soft morning light. It was a gradual awakening, more like the steady unfolding of a flower in blossom than a sudden realization. Spending time with him seemed to strengthen our bond till it was unbreakable, and I felt a warmth radiating from the core of my being.

I could clearly see my own feelings reflected back at me as I looked into his eyes. It was a love that seemed sweet and lasting, and it went beyond simple infatuation. And when he said he loved me, the words lingered in the atmosphere, enveloping us in a consoling hug.

Right then, I knew I was in love. His words echoed in my head, making me happy. His voice rang true as he cried back, "I LOVE YOU TOO!" Knowing that the man I loved felt the same way about me was a great moment.

Our love wasn't simple, though. We had to move stealthily, seizing our time together behind closed doors. It was impossible to go on dates because my grandparents would never be on board. I would be shut up in the house and kept away from him if they found out.

I choose to play it cool and wear a mask of indifference to hide my feelings. But every day that went by, it got more difficult for me to control my emotions. They erupted inside of me, ready to explode at any second.

I reached a point when I was unable to hide it. I had an urge to tell people about it, so I told my grandmother about it, knowing that she would disapprove. She handled it better than I thought, actually. Maybe it was because my grandfather was quickly admitted to a nursing home due to his deteriorating health.

The dynamics at home changed after my grandfather was admitted to the nursing home. I discovered that I was taking on more duties and making up for the gaps left by his absence. I had to start doing things like taking care of our animals and mowing the grass. Trying to hold everything together throughout the upheaval of my grandfather's illness was a difficult load to bear.

But in spite of all the difficulties, our love became deeper. As a bright point in the middle of chaos, our stolen moments become even more valuable. And he was there for me the entire time, lending his understanding and support.

Looking back on those turbulent days, I see that love always manages to overcome hardship. Even though it's not always simple, it's something to strive for. Furthermore, love has the ability to illuminate our path even in the darkest of circumstances.

After some time, my grandfather left the nursing home and came home. Things appeared to be improving at first. For a few weeks, he was doing wonderfully well, and we treasured those priceless weeks spent together. However, he suddenly became sick once more and needed to be taken to the hospital.

Our family was going through a trying period as we struggled with the unknown of his illness. The sad news that my grandfather had cancer was conveyed by the doctors despite our expectations for his recovery. His health issues were made more complicated by his battle with diabetes as if that weren't enough.

As I watched him struggle to free himself from the crippling hold of disease, my heart hurt. Although he was a strong and resilient man, even the most formidable fighters had their limitations. He was a source of strength and kindness for our family, even in the face of illness.

We gathered by his bedside in the last few days, trying to console him in every way we could. I was overcome with memories of his kind smile, his infectious laughter, and the innumerable times we spent together. He had been my rock and my source of unwavering love and support for everything.

And so, surrounded by his family's love, we said our final goodbyes to him with heavy hearts as he went away quietly. At the same time, as we were really grateful for the time we had spent with him, there was also a great deal of sadness.

I couldn't help but be thankful for the memories we had made together even as we grieved his passing. Even though he left us too young, his soul will always be a part of our hearts. For me, he was more than just a grandfather; he was a wellspring of courage, insight, and unfailing love.

Even though my grandfather passed away, his legacy will live on as a reminder of what a remarkable guy he was. Every person he encountered was impacted by him, and he left behind a loving and compassionate legacy that will motivate us going forward.

To me, my grandfather was more than just a grandfather—he was a father figure. He was an important part of my mother's and my two sisters' upbringing, along with my grandma. They performed an amazing job of giving us stability, love, and direction.

I got the impression that time had stopped when my grandfather died. His loss had left me in excruciating pain, and my sadness was nearly unbearable. I found it difficult to accept that he was no longer with us and that his soothing presence and pleasant smile would always be missed.

Your father began to reach out to me when I was in the middle of my grief. My grandmother would answer the phone whenever he called, screaming that he was on the line for me with an urgent tone in her voice. She tried to get us together, but I just couldn't bring myself to talk to him.

It was hard for me to find the right words to express the grief I carried within me, like a huge burden. His voice served as a bitter reminder of what I had lost each time I heard it. I wanted to withdraw from the outside world, wallow in my sorrow, and protect myself from further harm.

It wasn't that I didn't value your father's attempts to get in touch with me. I knew he was thinking of me, that he wanted to console me in this trying moment. However, the anguish was still too intense and recent for me to interact with him in a significant manner.

Rather, I turned inward, blocking off the outside world and concentrating only on my sorrow. I had no idea how to put into words the magnitude of my suffering or the emptiness I was experiencing on the inside. Because I couldn't let your dad in while I was still processing my own feelings, I pushed him away.

I see now, looking back, that cutting him off was a mistake. In an extremely tough moment, your dad was attempting to support and console me. However, I was in such a state of sadness that I was unable to look past my own suffering and appreciate the love and care he was providing.

I still feel bad about pushing away someone who was merely trying to be of assistance. However, I was so overcome with grief that I was unable to see past the shadows to recognize his compassion. And I will always be sorry for that.

I started writing as a coping mechanism for the sadness of losing my grandfather. Writing turned become a means of escape for me, allowing me to release my feelings and find comfort in the written words. I stayed indoors for a time, not being able to share my feelings with your dad or anybody else.

I began to rediscover who I was as time went on. As my pain started to lessen, I started to yearn for your dad's presence once again. I wanted him close by, to give me the solace and encouragement that only he could.

However, I never got a response when I tried to get in touch with him. I would leave message after message on his phone, waiting for a response that never materialized since his phone would go directly to voicemail.

I felt like I was shouting into space and no one was listening, which was a depressing and unpleasant experience. I yearned to get back in touch with your dad and close the distance that had grown between us during my lowest points.

However, I never got a response, regardless of how many messages I left or how many times I tried to call. I had the impression that he had vanished from my life, leaving me to deal with my loss on my own once more.

When all I wanted was for him to be by my side, I didn't understand why he was avoiding me and acting as like he was shutting me out. The idea that he might be pulling away from me and not caring about what I was going through hurt.

I was hurt by his quiet, but I didn't give up hope. I kept trying to get in touch with him, hoping that eventually he would return my calls and we could be back together.

I recall the day I went to the lake to find comfort after calling your dad a thousand times. I ended up sitting at the water's edge and daydreaming about fishing trips with my grandfather because I needed to get away from the weight of my emotions and clear my thoughts.

Your dad seemed to materialize out of nowhere as I sat there, lost in nostalgia. In my hour of need, his presence was a consoling embrace as he sat down next to me. He hugged me tightly without saying anything, his arms providing the comfort and security I had been missing.

He whispered, "I missed you," with a genuine tone in his voice. And at that very moment, all of the suffering and yearning I had been holding inside of me spilled out in tears.

There beside the lake, we had hours of uninterrupted discourse during which we freely exchanged our feelings and thoughts. Your dad expressed his sadness for not being there to support me during such a trying time and apologized for missing my grandfather's burial.

And then, in a vulnerable moment, he made a promise that excited me and gave me hope. He said, "You're going to be my wife when you turn eighteen," with such seriousness that it stopped me cold.

I experienced a wave of happiness and thankfulness at that precise time. Being aware of his desire to wed me and live out the rest of his days beside me, gave me a feeling of purpose and belonging that I had never experienced before. I grinned, fully believing what he had said.

I was incredibly fortunate to have discovered someone who genuinely loved me and was prepared to support me no matter what. I also knew that no matter what obstacles were ahead, we would overcome them together, hand in hand, as we sat there together, watching the sunset over the lake.

I gained the courage to trust in love once more and in the prospect of a happy and fulfilled future in your dad's embrace. And while we sat there together, I realized that our love was indeed unique and that I should cling to it with all of my heart.

Chapter 3

Life is never a straight path; it is filled with ups and downs. You can never be sure of what is heading your way. But as time passes, you eventually start to realize who is in your life for real, who was never there for you, and those special ones who are there for you no matter what. I learned this lesson the hard way.

Understanding that life is more than just being alive in a fantasy world took some time for me. I have to accept reality and grow up. My heart found it difficult to embrace what my intellect knew to be true.

I clung to hope for three long years, waiting to be with and love your dad. I thought all my wishes would come true when he finally told me he wanted to marry me. However, after that, things altered.

He seemed to vanish from my life once he made that vow. He ceased communicating with me, and I had the impression that I was abandoned in the dark. I was overcome with grief and plagued by visions of our shared past.

I was immersed in a sea of sadness and embarked on a solitary and agonizing trip. I was baffled as to why he had abruptly disappeared, and it led me to hope for a future that would never materialize.

I was on the verge of losing everything one day because the anguish was too great to handle. I took too many pain pills, hoping to escape from the overwhelming grief that consumed me. I even realized that I was abusing alcohol in a last-ditch effort to dull the hurt of missing your dad. It was a difficult period, with many nights spent sobbing in an attempt to block out the emptiness in my heart.

But then, after what seemed like a lifetime, your father got in touch with me. He desired to see and speak with me. We therefore, made plans to meet by the lake, a location that was very special to us. My heart ached with anticipation and fear as I waited for him to arrive.

When he finally did show up, I got overwhelmed with emotion. I started to feel angry, resentful, and upset when I challenged him about his absence. I let out all of my pent-up emotions by shouting because I was unable to control the tsunami of emotions that had been rising inside of me for so long.

And then, your dad got down on one knee in a way that totally took me by surprise. The words "Will you marry me?" that I had been waiting to hear from him since I first fell in love stopped my heart.

As I tried to make sense of everything, it seemed like time had stopped. The last few years of crazy passed and were replaced by a wave of disbelief and happiness. I screamed "YES" with all the joy and excitement I could summon, tears welling up in my eyes.

Everything changed the moment he slid the ring onto my finger. My shoulders were freed from the burden of the past, and I was filled with opportunity and hope for the future. We kissed, lost in the moment and our intense love for one another as he raised me up in his arms.

I realized that we were intended to be together despite the difficulties we had encountered as we embraced each other closely. After enduring many hardships, our love had become stronger and more resilient than before.

And as we turned to face the path ahead of us, I couldn't help but be appreciative of the twists that had led us to this point. In the end, love overcomes hardship, demonstrating that there is always hope for a better tomorrow, even in the darkest of circumstances.

I was constantly surprised by your dad's ways. He seemed to be living in a secret world that not even his own family was aware of. They had no idea that I existed at all, not even that my name was Katie.

It was an intimidating experience the first time I went to Louisiana to meet his folks. I recall the wonderful smell of food cooking in the kitchen when

I first entered their house. While your dad's mother was occupied with cooking, he used the occasion to welcome me to his family.

I was somewhat anxious. Meeting his parents for the first time felt like a big step, and I wasn't sure what to expect. Still, they gave me a cordial welcome when I arrived at their home. I felt a surge of relief go over me. Their kindness and friendliness put me at ease from the start.

Although I was first anxious, my visit was a wonderful experience. Since your dad's family received me as one of their own, I felt like I belonged from the time I walked through the door.

As we ate together, I couldn't help but be grateful for the opportunity to get to know them better. It was a chance to deepen our relationship and lay the foundation for our future collaboration.

Now that I'm thinking back on that day, I see how important it was for us to meet your dad's relatives. It demonstrated the sincerity of our love and our readiness to move forward as a couple despite the difficulties that may lie ahead.

And as I think back on the journey that has brought us this far, I can't help but feel grateful for the love and support of your dad's family. They welcomed me into their lives with open arms, and for that I will always be thankful.

There was an appeal to your dad that was difficult to ignore. And his parents exhibited the same warmth and friendliness as he did. Together, we sat down to a wonderful dinner that your dad's mother had cooked. We laughed and told stories while we ate.

Your dad and I made the decision to explore the neighboring Gator town after supper. There were many fascinating sights to witness, including actual alligators, during the thrilling experience. Since we had recently gotten engaged, it seemed like a true date because it was our first time going out in public together.

We strolled hand in hand, enjoying everything that the Gator village had to offer as we marveled at its sights and sounds. We had a unique opportunity to spend time together without any concerns or interruptions, so it was quite memorable.

I couldn't help but feel contentment and happiness sweep over me as we went around the village. It felt like everything was coming together at last after years of waiting and hoping for this moment.

We then decided on a wedding date as we made our way back home. I will always remember that day, which was brimming with excitement and anticipation, as we were ready to begin our lives as husband and wife.

As I reflect on that occasion, I see how unique and significant it was. When we seized the opportunity to publicly declare our love and dedication to one another in front of friends and family, our relationship experienced a radical transformation.

Upon reflection of the path that led us here, I am overwhelmed with gratitude for every second we spent together. Every moment of our journey together, from the day we first met to our wedding, has been joyous, lighthearted, and loving. And I have no doubt that as we spend each day together on our journey, our love will only grow.

We decided to get married at the Methodist Church of Bedias on May 5, 2012. I was so excited that I could not wait to start planning our wedding day decorations. In order to guarantee that every little thing would be ideal, we even bought a cake from one of the best florists in the area.

Finally, my grandmother got me a gorgeous wedding dress from College Station, Texas, that was marked down. It was a stunning masterpiece, all white and red velvet. The dress was really stunning, with a lengthy train that flowed behind me. I was overcome with delight and happiness as soon as I put the gown on for the first time. I had a wave of happiness, as I stood there, overwhelmed by the dress's loveliness. I had been dreaming of this moment, and now it was finally coming true.

My shape was exquisitely hugged in all the right areas by the gown. Dancing in front of the mirror, I twirled and enjoyed the way the fabric clung to me. It seemed fanciful, and I was in disbelief that I was the bride in this enchanted tale.

Gratitude for my family's love and support overwhelmed me as I stared in the mirror at the stunning gown my grandmother had purchased for me. This was a memorable experience that I will always treasure because of their generosity.

I knew that our wedding day would be remarkable since I was overcome with love and joy. In my wedding gown, ready to embark on our adventure as husband and wife in front of our loved ones, I was eager to write the next chapter in our love story.

As I got ready to tie the knot with the love of my life, I couldn't hide how happy I was. I scheduled the Civic Center for the reception following the wedding and sent out all of the invites. I spent a lot of time with my family decorating the space to make sure it was ideal for our special day.

But when the big day for the wedding finally arrived, anxiety took precedence over my excitement. In an attempt to provide some comfort and reduce my anxiousness, I kept phoning to see if he was in town. But no matter how often I called, neither he nor any of my family members answered. He appeared to have disappeared out of thin air.

My nervousness increased as the hours passed. I had a persistent sense that something wasn't right. Then, as the ceremony's time approached, it became painfully obvious that he would not be attending. I was left standing by myself at the altar, surrounded by broken dreams and empty chairs.

It had all been for naught, all that work and planning. My heart was full of excitement and expectation as the site was set up and invites were sent out. However, it was all in vain in the end.

My disappointment washed over me when I realized that my wedding day had been a letdown.

My beloved and the guy I was meant to wed had silently deserted me, leaving me to deal with the shame and anguish on my own.

I couldn't help but feel deceived and abandoned at that very moment. My mind was filled with questions. How could he do this to me? How could he, on the day that was destined to be the happiest day of my life, leave me standing all alone there by myself, heartbroken?

It was meant to be a day of pure love and happiness, but instead, it was turned into a dark reminder of the heartbreak and uncertainty that come with being in love with someone who is untrustworthy.

I was shattered and found myself falling deep into desolation as the reality of being let down on my wedding day set in. I was lost as to why I had to go through this heart wrenching experience. If he couldn't make it to the wedding, why couldn't he at least give me a call to let me know? My feelings for him were gradually fading and being replaced by hurt and a sense of betrayal. My heart was hit by a devastating blow, and I was unable to control the intense feelings that washed over me.

I cried uncontrollably, asking my grandmother and sisters for moral support and why this had happened to me. They were there to provide me with consoling words and a shoulder to weep on in my hour of need.

However, despite their assistance, I was still having trouble processing what had transpired. I was adrift and confused, looking for answers that didn't seem to be forthcoming to me.

I started writing as a way to vent my desperation. I used to write messages to balloons, attach them with words that conveyed my suffering and perplexity, and watch them take off into the sky. I was able to release my feelings and send my thoughts into the cosmos in the hopes of coming to some sort of resolution.

In my letters, I also begged God to return so he could explain why he wasn't present on our wedding day and begged for answers. My letters were naked expressions of my anguish and longing, a frantic plea for comprehension in the middle of chaos.

And when I ran out of things to say, I would go outside and shout until the night sky opened up, tears streaming down my cheeks. I was able to let out my frustrations and pain in the face of unbearable sadness through this primordial release of pent-up emotion.

I felt like I was drowning in grief during those gloomy days. But despite everything, I held onto the hope that I would eventually find comfort and healing. And even though I knew I had my family's love and support to help me recover from this dreadful event, I knew I would finally make it back to the shore.

I felt like I was driving through life aimlessly, not knowing where I was heading or what to do next. I felt hollow and empty inside, and the pain of being turned down on my wedding day weighed heavily on my heart. It appeared as though there was no way out of the terrifying experience. I could not admit to myself that it had really happened, try as I may.

One day, though, my grandmother recommended that we go to lunch with a friend of hers who was in town. Even though it was a straightforward invitation, it gave me a ray of optimism amid the clouds of uncertainty in my thoughts. Grateful for the diversion from my own concerns, I jumped into the car with her without any hesitation.

We were driving into town when I became lost in thought, trying to make sense of the swirling, turbulent feelings inside of me. However, as the miles passed, my excitement level increased. Perhaps having lunch with my grandma's friend would provide me with the much-needed respite from the pain and despair that were weighing so heavily on my heart.

I was surprised to see your dad waiting there with flowers when we got to the lunch spot. He was kneeling again, this time in prayer rather than in proposal, asking for another opportunity. It looked like a scene from a movie. I felt like I was in a tornado, alternating between perplexity and rage.

I knew, however, that I needed answers. I had a right to know the reason behind his betrayal on our wedding day. I gave him the benefit of the doubt and let him talk. To my further perplexity, he informed me that he had been in the hospital. I wasn't sure if I should believe him. It seems overly handy and fortuitous.

A part of me wanted to ignore him, to cut him off because of the suffering he had brought about. However, there was a gentler side of me that yearned to think that there might be forgiveness and healing.

His statements were genuine and full of real emotion as he begged me to give him another opportunity. He said, "I love you," his grasp getting tighter. He revealed a vulnerable side to his feelings for me in that fleeting time.

And I found myself caving into his entreaties in spite of my better sense. My heart seemed to be acting on its own initiative, drawn in by his regret and love. Against all the odds, I decided to give him another chance and to let forgiveness and healing be a possibility in my heart.

Upon reflection, I can see that this was a crucial moment in our relationship. It was a time of forgiveness and grace, a chance to repair what had been broken. And I knew that if we faced the many challenges ahead together, we would come out stronger than before, despite the fact that there would be many. Even though I was still hurting, I found myself saying yes to your dad's getaway plan. We spent a beach weekend in Galveston, Texas. Although it was a kind gesture, I couldn't get over the hurt I was feeling.

The sound of breaking waves and the briny breeze welcomed us to the beach. Even though the environment was lovely, I still felt a lot of unresolved feelings in my heart. I was never able to forget the pain he had inflicted, even though he tried to make things right.

Together, we explored Galveston's landmarks and took walks along the shoreline over the whole weekend. Your dad tried his hardest to show me a nice time, but the scars from our past continued to follow him around.

It was an event that was both happy and humorous at the same time, but it was laced with disappointment and betrayal. I wanted to think that he was using this vacation to show me how much he cared and how much he loved me. However, I knew deep down that I was stuck with the questions and worries that were bothering me.

I struggled with my emotions in the days and weeks that followed, caught between wanting to forgive and not wanting to get wounded again. It was a challenging trip with many highs and lows as I tried to make sense of my feelings and figure out how to move forward.

One thing, though, was constant throughout it all: beneath the layers of hurt and disappointment, there was still the love I had for your dad. I was also prepared to go above and beyond to bring our relationship back together, even if it would require some time and work to mend the damage.

Following a turbulent path filled with pain and forgiveness, your father asked me once more if I would like to marry him. I was unsure of whether I could trust him not to break my heart again, so it was a moment of both anxiety and hope. However, I still harbored feelings for him, and I yearned for the opportunity to restore what we had lost.

I informed him that the only way I would consent to marry him was if he promised never to put me up against my will ever again. It was a straightforward request, but it was burdened by all the suffering and disappointment we had experienced. To my relief, he promised not to disappoint me once more and consented without hesitation.

We started organizing our wedding again, full of resolve and hope. We chose the same venues as before and, this time established the date for July 28, 2012. It seemed as if we had a second shot at happiness and could change how our love story ended.

It was only during our wedding preparations that your dad decided to inform his family of our intentions. It was a time of finally being recognized as a significant aspect of his life, and of validation. And as we took in their blessings and good wishes, I experienced a wave of relief and thankfulness.

I was filled with emotion on the day of our wedding as I made my way down the aisle toward your dad. I had been dreaming about this moment of unadulterated bliss and delight for a very long time. And I knew that this was the place I was supposed to be as we exchanged rings and vows in front of our loved ones.

Our wedding day was even better than I could have imagined. It was an expression of love and dedication and proof of how strong our relationship is. And I felt like the luckiest person alive as we danced the night away, engrossed in one another's arms.

Your dad had a way of making me feel like the girl I was when I fell in love with him, bringing out the best in me. He made me remember all the reasons I had initially fallen in love with him, and I will always be appreciative of that.

Chapter 4

After our hectic wedding, San Antonio's colorful allure drew us here for our honeymoon. Our days were full of romance as we wandered hand in hand and took in the vibrant energy of the city, nestled along the gorgeous Riverwalk. We had dinner at a charming restaurant one evening, enjoying every meal and raising a glass to our recently joined lives. One day, we went to a wax museum and were astonished by the lifelike sculptures that gave the impression of travelling us back in time. We clasped to each other closely as we made our way through the eerie hallways of a haunted house because, of course, we were thrill-seekers and couldn't resist its charm.

Then, without any warning or explanation, he disappeared into the night, and left me all alone by myself in the hotel room that we had picked out especially for our weekend retreat. Minutes felt like hours as I waited for him to come back to me. I kept waiting and he didn't come back. He finally made his way back to the room past midnight and it was almost three in the morning. Oh, it was too much for me to handle. The wrath was boiling up inside of me! It wasn't even long after our marriage that he began to act mysteriously like way. I wondered what had gone wrong, but it felt like the ink on our marriage license had hardly dry before he was out on his own.

My formerly bright future with him started to fade as we traveled back to Louisiana, my new home state. Transitioning to life with his parents was a temporary fix that quickly became apparent to have its drawbacks. I was looking for relief from the oppressive limitations of our current circumstance, so I turned to the glow of the computer screen during one of his long workdays.

I searched the internet for reasonably priced apartments in our neighborhood, driven by a strong sense of need to find us a place of our own. Every click felt like a step closer to freedom, a ray of hope amid the darkness that felt like it was about to swallow us. I couldn't help but feel a wave of empowerment running through my veins as I combed through listing after listing, seeing the possibilities of a new beginning.

Yes, I did happen upon a Baton Rouge apartment that drew my attention. It seemed like a reasonable choice for us. To be sure I could show your dad later, I mentally noted the URL of the webpage where I discovered it. Weary after the day's work, I quickly opened the computer screen and showed him the apartment listing. Reading the details peaked his interest. We made the snap decision to get in touch with the landlords and arrange a visit. It felt like a tiny triumph in our trip, a glimmer of hope amid the clouds of doubt.

We were getting closer to establishing a home we could call our own, a haven from the chaos around us, with every step we took. We therefore started the next chapter of our lives, excited to explore where this newfound chance would take us, equipped with resolve and a feeling of purpose.

We enthusiastically set out to see the apartment in person the very following day after scheduling the visit. As soon as we entered, we took our time looking around every corner and imagining our lives taking place within. We quickly came to the conclusion that this was the location we wanted to call home. So we decided to move in without second thought. We occupied ourselves during the next few weeks with packing, arranging, and getting ready for the big move. And by the time October 2012 came around, we had made our way happily into our new home. The humble home that we called ours was more than just an apartment to us it was a symbol of our commitment to each other and the start of our journey together as a family.

Oh, the happiness we experienced that day! I remember that day very clearly, the first time we set foot in our new house. All over, there were boxes piled high, waiting to be opened and turned into comfortable spaces. We took a moment to appreciate the importance of the occasion despite the turmoil of moving. Our living room floor was bare when we sat down to spend a straightforward yet meaningful moment together. We took in the breathtaking view outside the large window while sipping glasses of wine. It was a moment in time captured in a still image of unadulterated happiness. We were so full of appreciation and excitement for the adventures at that very time, surrounded by the possibility of fresh starts.

We were lucky to get the apartment building's top story. With the city below, we felt as though we were alone on top of the entire world. Our love exploded at that same moment, and we made love to each other. We shared a love that was stronger than words and could not be contained by anything; it was evident in every touch and kiss. A melding of souls united by the cords of love, it was a moment of absolute intimacy. We also knew that this moment would be ingrained in our memories for all time, as we lay there, entwined in each other's embrace.

Halloween drew near as the days went on, and we enthusiastically embraced its festive mood. Together, we decked out our new place with eerie décor to turn it into a fun sanctuary filled with Halloween treats. Working together to create our first Halloween gingerbread house was one of the season's highlights. It was funny to watch your dad, who is normally so calm, get upset over the fine details of our adorable creation. His impatience with such delicate activities added a lightheartedness to the occasion, making our home a joyful and laughing place.

We learned more about one other every day as we navigated our new life together. The next day, your dad got home from work and found not one, but two Pomeranian dogs. That was one unexpected surprise. It was a nice surprise to see him enter the room accompanied by the cute couple. The mother of the energetic and inquisitive puppy was one of them, and the other was a gentle and kind puppy. Their wagging tails and joyful activities immediately filled our home with warmth and affection, making us happy. Even though the gesture was unexpected, we couldn't resist falling in love with our new furry friends.

And let's not overlook my dear cocktail bird, my loyal companion from my Texas days. He was a continual source of joy and chirps, adding a little symphony from nature to our house. We also had two baby water turtles that I was responsible for caring for alongside him. With their small shells and cute antics, these little creatures brought their own special charm to our home.

To make our pets feel completely at home, your dad went above and above. He surprised me by setting up a huge area with lots of room for our turtles to swim and explore. Furthermore, he made them a comfortable area to lounge beneath a heat lamp. That was such a kind act, and it filled our tiny family up. We were ecstatic to have all of our animals together under one roof. With its constant chirps, splashes, and the sporadic rustle of small wings, it resembled our own little zoo.

However, my life took an unexpected turn, and when I found out I was pregnant with you, it became 10 times more amazing! I'll never forget how my appetite changed and I started to feel incredibly nauseous. In addition, I observed that my monthly cycles weren't occurring as they typically did. As the news that I would be a mother began to sink in, my emotions went into overdrive.

So, I decided to take a pregnancy test just to be sure. When the result flashed "pregnant," I was filled with a mix of excitement and nervousness. The thought of becoming a mommy filled my heart with joy, but it also brought a wave of uncertainty about the journey ahead. I couldn't wait to share the news with your dad when he returned home. The anticipation bubbled inside me as I imagined his reaction to the life-changing news. It was a moment

I had been dreaming of, picturing the look of happiness and surprise on his face.

I made a nice meal and set a romantic mood for the two of us. My pulse raced with excitement as I heard him get closer to our apartment. I surprised him with dinner when he arrived and, more importantly, told him the big news. When I told him we were expecting a baby, his excitement was genuine. He was so happy that he started bouncing across the room with excitement. He was ecstatic. Observing his response made me feel incredibly happy and satisfied. We cheered and welcomed the path ahead as soon-to-be parents together, and it was an absolutely beautiful moment. The love and excitement that filled the room were palpable, a testament to the strength of our bond and the excitement of starting this new chapter in our lives.

Dinner was completely forgotten in the momentous excitement. Your dad said, "Let's go!" his eyes glistening with excitement. I must tell my parents during dinner. He could barely contain his excitement as the news broke. He didn't think twice to give his brother the amazing news that he was going to become an uncle! His zeal was contagious, bubbling over with every word uttered. He could not wait to tell his parents the news; he was determined not to wait another second.

We hurriedly called his parents to ask them to come over immediately for a surprise, as we were so excited about the occasion. We all sat down together in a Mexican restaurant in Gonzales, LA. I was getting morning sickness, so I hurried to the bathroom as soon as I felt nauseous. It was an unplanned diversion, but in a second I was back at the table, trying not to show my discomfort. Still, his mom already knew I was pregnant. As we sat there together, excited to tell his parents about our surprise, the anticipation and joy persisted despite the unanticipated turn of events.

Your dad broke the news with a broad smile on his face, unable to control his excitement: "We're pregnant! You will become grandparents." I wasn't sure how his mom felt about the announcement, but his dad's face brightened up with joy. She told me, "You two had only recently gotten married," with a hint of hesitation in her voice. Why wait to start a family?" I was taken aback by her remarks and saw a trace of worry in her voice.

His mom was always the quiet type, but she had her own gentle way of showing kindness. Despite her reserved nature, she had a sweetness about her that shone through in subtle ways. On the other hand, your dad's father was quite the character - a man who always seemed to have the final say in any conversation. He had a commanding presence and a knack for asserting his opinions with authority.

For us, being pregnant with you changed everything. We were all excitedly waiting for you to arrive when I observed your dad changing too. Oh, and I had different cravings when I was pregnant! Day or night, I could not get enough ice cream. I started to crave it constantly and would indulge whenever I could. Every time your dad got home from work, I used to tell him, "Let's go to Sonic!" They have an enormous variety of ice cream flavors." It therefore became a small ritual for us. Almost every evening, we would visit Sonic to try out all of their delectable ice cream flavors.

It's funny how ice cream, something so basic, can take on such a significant role in your pregnancy. It was more than simply a hunger for me; it was a source of solace, a means of indulging my sweet taste and adding a little happiness to every day. And your dad, God bless him, was always up for going out for ice cream with me at night.

We both got more and more excited as the weeks went by and my belly got bigger. We dreamed for hours about what life would be like with you and all the family adventures we would go on. And all the while, ice cream stayed a constant, a delicious memento of the adventure we were taking together.

Now that I'm looking back, some of my favorite memories of being pregnant with you are those late-night trips to Sonic. It was more than simply the ice cream, though that was a tasty side dish, too. It was about the time we had together, cherishing every second and looking forward to the day we could finally embrace you. Everything else vanished as we sat there together in the brightness of the neon lights. It was just the two of us, engrossed in the thrill and expectation of becoming parents. We couldn't wait to start this new journey with you by our side, even if we weren't precisely sure what the future held.

It was finally time for my doctor's appointment, and I headed in to get everything checked out. I was feeling really anxious, especially about finding out your gender. Of course, your dad's parents were there in the room with us. When the ultrasound lady said, "It's a girl," we all burst with excitement! It was such a special moment, knowing what you were going to be. There was a mix of emotions in the room - joy, excitement, and maybe even a little bit of surprise. But above all, there was a feeling of love and anticipation as we eagerly awaited your arrival. That day marked a milestone in our journey as parents-to-be, and it was a memory we would cherish forever.

After some time passed and we learned we were expecting a girl, everything started to change again. Your grandparents had always longed for a granddaughter, so they were ecstatic and happy beyond words. For them, finding out that I was pregnant with you was like a dream come true. We could feel their joy, and it quickly swept through our family. Their excitement at finally having a little girl in the family warmed my heart.

We had incredible adventures as we eagerly anticipated your arrival. In an effort to outfit you in the finest, we lavished on designer clothing for you. To make sure everything was ideal for you, we even chose a stunning bedroom set for your space. At the prospect of bringing our lovely baby daughter into the world, we felt as though we were on cloud nine, bursting with happiness and expectation. We poured our love and passion into making this place cozy and welcoming for you at every turn. Making you the happiest young child on the planet was our only goal. Our hearts grew fonder and more excited as we browsed shops and selected items for your nursery. We couldn't wait to see your sweet face and hold you in our arms, knowing that you would bring us endless joy and happiness.

Chapter 5

After settling everything and getting everything we needed for you, we began to make further arrangements. I had a long conversation with your dad about buying a house so you could have a room of your own. We had visions of your bedroom as a warm and inviting place with all the adorable little butterfly decorations we had carefully chosen. The tiny butterfly designs were specifically picked to create a whimsical and tranquil environment for you. They come in pastel and vivid tones. A house with two bedrooms—one tastefully furnished for you and the other for your dad and me—was now all we needed. We couldn't wait to see you tucked away in your own unique space, surrounded by everything we had chosen with such care.

Of course, our intention was to have you in our bedroom from the moment of your birth, so that you could be beside us. It was nice to know that you were close by, so we could simply take care of all of your needs. We were aware, nevertheless, that our one-bedroom apartment was insufficient for raising a family. We desired for you to have room to develop and explore, as well as a place where each day would be an occasion to celebrate and enjoy your presence.

I have complete confidence in stating that your dad has never missed one of my doctor's appointments. He never left my side, never wavered in his love or support. He shared in every moment of excitement and anticipation as each appointment brought them one step closer to finally meeting you. Like a good father would, he took me to all of them, making sure that you and I were taken care of. His obvious devotion and hard work gave me a great sense of gratitude and comfort.

Then, my darling, arrived the moment you were about to be born—the happiest day of my life. We had been excitedly awaiting your arrival for months, and the countdown to your arrival was approaching. We were thrilled and in awe of every kick and movement you made inside of me. We were getting ready, both mentally and physically, for the day when we would finally be able to embrace you.

To see you, my grandmother and two of my cousins traveled from Texas. Despite the length of their journey, it was all worth it because of their joy at meeting you. It was evidence of how much affection there was for you even before you were born. Their faces beaming with excitement and anticipation, as we got ready for your arrival, they arrived right on schedule.

There's another reason the day of your birth was remarkable. The same day I went to deliver you, your aunt, my middle sister, went into labor as well. The fact that two of our new family members would be born so soon after, sharing not only the same birthdate but also the same hour, was a bizarre coincidence. It's true that your cousin and you were born six minutes apart. Our family experienced twice the happiness in a single day, as if the cosmos had come together to do so.

Tears streamed down my cheeks as I finally got to hold you in my arms for the first time. The feelings were too much to handle. You were adorable in every manner possible for a baby. I recall squinting down at your little face, which seemed so innocent and unseasoned. You were even cuter to me because of the detail of your ice cream cone-shaped head. In a few days, as the doctor had promised, it will return to a more normal shape, so we need not be alarmed. However, at the time, I thought it was the greatest thing ever—a particular little detail that added even more significance to your early moments.

You were such a blessing to us. You have filled our life with so much love and happiness right from the start. I also recall the day, just before we left the hospital, when we dressed you all in white. We wanted everything to be ideal for your first trip home because it was a unique moment. Your dad's mother, your grandma, had chosen the most exquisite ensemble for you in the shopping center. It was a beautiful white garment with tiny embroidered flowers and lovely lace trimmings. The outfit was completed with an elegant touch that made you look like a tiny angel, and the matching shoes were equally exquisite. She had also selected a charming tiny white bonnet to go with the garment, which gave it even more beauty. I hugged you close as we got ready to leave the hospital, thinking of how adorable you looked in your new clothes. As we prepared everything for the trip home and grabbed your stuff, the hospital room was a flurry of activity and enthusiasm. The nurses stopped over to congratulate you, and several even said you looked stunning in your dress. Their complimentary remarks made me feel proud and content.

Holding you tenderly in my arms, I was pushed outside on the wheelchair. It was overwhelming to have you so close and to know that we were going to begin a new chapter in our lives together. Your father strolled next to us, his eyes fixed on you the entire time, beaming with happiness and pure love. Your grandfather was excited to see you and take you home as soon as we arrived at the hospital's exit.

But your dad and his dad got into a little fight about who was going to drive us home. They both forgot what was truly important since they were both so happy and anxious to be the ones to bring you home. I sat there holding you as they argued, thinking to myself that it didn't matter who drove as long as we all made it home without incident. Being with you and making sure you were safe and comfortable was my top priority.

Your dad and I brought you home, and his parents followed closely behind. I just wanted to lay down with you by my side because I was so exhausted. However, that did not occur. Your father held you close to his parents. Following the hospital, both my grandmother and my cousins departed. Before they would allow me to leave the hospital, I had to spend one night there with you. I was still there when they left that evening, and the following day we were released. All I wanted was to be with you, to hold you, but they were always there, so I couldn't. It was fine at first, but soon after that they began to visit frequently.

I didn't fully understand the changes my body and mind were going through when I gave birth to you because I was so young. With your arrival, postpartum depression sneaked into my life, and I'm still not sure why. Maybe it was the weight of everything your dad and I were going through, the seemingly never-ending struggles. Or perhaps it was just the heavy burden of becoming a mother at such a young age. For whatever reason, my mind turned into a war zone of opposing feelings.

I was filled with uncertainties, doubting my capacity to care for and shield you from my own turmoil. My mind was filled with thoughts, each one scarier than the last. However, one thing held true despite all of the chaos: my undying love for you, my precious child.

I went to a counselor in need of comfort and direction. In my lowest points, their wise counsel served as a lifeline and a beacon of hope amidst the chaos. They helped me face the demons that threatened to consume me as I set out on a healing journey.

Medication turned into a vital weapon in my fight against postpartum depression, a ray of hope amid the darkness. I persisted despite the difficulties, driven by a strong will to vanquish this unseen enemy and take back my life.

You were my rock throughout it all, a constant source of courage and motivation in the face of difficulty. I kept you close, finding solace in the warmth of your hug, understanding that there was innocence in you.

I was deeply hurt by your dad's accusations, which left me stunned and doubting my capacity to be a mother. I can still clearly recall the yard sale incident, which served as a sobering reminder of the extent he would go to in order to challenge my authority.

I remember the crisp morning air tinged with the promise of autumn, and me pushing your tiny body around in the stroller on our way to the neighbor's yard sale. With just you and me and a quiet suburban street as the background, it was a serene moment. And yet your dad's unexpected arrival broke that peace in an instant.

I was caught off guard by his frenzied behavior, accusing me while he dragged you from the security of the stroller and drove off in his truck. He felt that I had been careless and had put your life in danger by letting you experience the purportedly oppressive heat of a cool autumn morning.

However, the reality was far from his inflated assertions. The neighborhood was enveloped in a warm glow as the sun started its ascent. It was a far cry from the searing heat he insisted upon, but he didn't seem to notice it because he was so focused on portraying me as unfit.

My heart ached from frustration and rage as he drove off with you in tow. How could he play you like a pawn in his devious game of manipulation and betray my trust with such callousness? And yet, there was a glimmer of fear even in the middle of my rage.

I sat in our home alone, the silence crushing me under my weight as I waited for him to come home with you. The hours went by slowly, with every minute seeming to drag on while I struggled with my mounting uneasiness. We could feel the tension building between us, like a storm approaching, when he eventually came back.

Our long-simmering resentment eventually erupted into a furious dispute as the evening went on. I felt vulnerable and abandoned without him, and I couldn't help but snap at him. But rather than comfort me, he responded to my words with rage, losing his cool and throwing my phone against the wall.

In that instant, the world seemed to come crashing down around me. You, my precious child, were mere inches away, your innocent eyes wide with confusion as you watched the chaos unfold. I was so young, so naive, unable to comprehend the gravity of the situation we found ourselves in.

I felt imprisoned in my own house and found it difficult to negotiate the rough seas of my relationship with your father. I had to tread carefully around him because of his volatile temper because I never knew when he would lose it. I can still clearly recall one specific instance that serves as a terrifying reminder of the depths of his rage. That was just another typical day, with the sun low in the sky as I went next door to escape the stuffy atmosphere of our own house. But rather than finding comfort, what I saw was a locked door with your tiny form peeking through the window while you played carelessly inside.

I felt a wave of panic come over me when I realized I was locked out and that my resentment and anger were keeping me from you. In need of assistance badly, I turned to our neighbors, whose generosity shone brightly in the shadows that were threatening to swallow me.

They immediately invited me into their home and provided me with consolation and assistance during my time of need. They insisted that I stay overnight, giving me a place to hide safe from the mayhem that pervaded our own four walls. They reassured me that I was welcome and that their generosity was a salve for my wounded soul, even though I was hesitant to demand their kindness.

That evening, as I relaxed in a warm bath, the stress gradually started to fade and was replaced by a calmness I hadn't experienced in a long time. But even as I basked in the easy joys of leisure, a persistent fear gnawed at the back of my mind.

It was a fear rooted in uncertainty, wondering what our family's future held. And even though our neighbors insisted that I call the police for assistance, I just couldn't bring myself to do it. I was afraid to think of calling the police because the consequences of taking such a drastic step were too horrible to consider.

So I slept in their guest room that night, struggling to find a way to feel both happy and sad. Ultimately, I made the decision to head back home the following day, holding out hope that the nightmare would soon end. However, I realized the fight was far from done as soon as I stepped through our front door.

Chapter 6

As time passed, living with your dad grew more and more difficult. When he started drinking excessively and going out late, his behavior took a troubling turn, and I started to worry a lot about both our relationship and his well-being. His parents were also usually unaware of his whereabouts, so I found myself constantly reaching out to them in the hopes of getting some closure or explanation. He seemed to be begging us to just keep our distance in order to remember the guy he once was.

There was a noticeable sense of anxiety in the air when he finally got home. It seemed like you were always treading on thin ice because you never knew when a simple comment might set off a chain reaction. I felt emotionally spent and alone since I had to constantly fight to deal with the erratic emotions and behaviors. I can still clearly remember the desperate moment I called my grandma and told her I wanted to get away from the stuffy environment at home.

We went to a marriage counselor as a last resort to try to save our collapsing marriage. But your Dad became really irate at the therapist's recommendations, which seemed to further aggravate the underlying problems during the session. I realized our marriage was on thin ice when he refused to participate in the process, which left me feeling helpless and defeated.

I had no choice but to make the painful choice to separate for a while. Though that wasn't what I had hoped for, it seemed like the only option left to keep my sanity and well-being intact.

Our home took on a different dynamic when my grandmother visited. My grandma decided to stay with us while her companion and her two kids remained at a neighboring motel. I was anxious for their company and support, so I welcomed their attendance in spite of your dad's misgivings.

I took the unorthodox choice to have your dad sleep on the couch and my grandma shares the bedroom with us in order to accommodate everyone. It was a modest action, but it represented my resolve to put my own wants and well-being first for once.

The next morning, when the sun came up, I was struggling with a choice that was very important to me. I took advantage of your dad's absence from work to confide in my grandmother and share my most intimate aspirations and anxieties. She quickly enlisted the help of her motel friend, and the two of us started the difficult process of packing up our lives.

Each thing we painstakingly packaged held a rush of memories, both happy and sad. My darling bird was a constant comfort to me during the turbulent days leading up to our departure, and I couldn't face the idea of leaving it behind in the midst of all the upheaval. Thus, in addition to necessities like clothing and possessions, we made sure my bird was securely tucked up for the trip ahead.

We traveled to an abuse shelter for women with heavy hearts, hoping to find safety from the storm that had taken over our lives. It was far from the warmth and coziness of home, a place of unfamiliarity and cold. There was a sense of satisfaction in knowing that we were finally free from your dad's toxic grip, while worry and uncertainty still lingered over us.

I let myself feel a glimmer of optimism at those isolated times when I cuddled you and spoke comforting whispers. For the first time in what seemed like a lifetime, I ventured to think of a better future—one in which we could reconstruct our lives free from your dad.

I had not experienced something as difficult as saying goodbye to my grandmother in a long time. Tears flowed down her cheeks as I hugged her closely, attempting to etch her warmth and love in my mind till our next meeting. She said, "I love you," as her voice faltered with emotion, and then she grudgingly got into the truck with her friend and her kids. I felt vulnerable and alone as a wave of melancholy swept over me as I watched them drive away.

My main objective became hiding from your dad, which gave me constant anxiety and fear. I couldn't get rid of the persistent fear that he would find us and pull us back into the chaotic environment from which we had fled. I therefore, continued to be watchful, keeping a low profile and avoiding any needless risks that could endanger our security and welfare.

In spite of all the difficulties and unknowns we faced, the refuge turned out to be a surprising source of comfort and assistance. I felt a sense of sisterhood and solidarity among the ladies that I was surrounded by, which had been sorely absent in my life. I made relationships with people who had traveled similar routes through conversations and shared experiences, and I found solace in their empathy and understanding.

91

But the thing that surprised us the most during our stay at the shelter was perhaps the sense of community that grew all around us. Individuals from all backgrounds gathered together, united by a common spirit of perseverance and resolve to surmount hardship. People fell in love with you and accepted you as one of their own, and in the middle of all the mayhem and uncertainty, I discovered unanticipated moments of happiness and connection.

Though it wasn't exactly as I had imagined things would work out, there was a glimmer of optimism for us that moment when we were surrounded by new friends and allies. I allowed myself to believe that happiness could be found even in the unlikeliest of places for the first time in a very long time.

I was given a little room in the shelter, a humble haven among the communal living areas. We shared the kitchen, living room, and bathroom with other women and their kids, so even though it offered some solitude, we still had to use the shared spaces. Even though we were in close quarters, there was a spirit of unity and a common awareness of the difficulties we were all facing.

I would take you to the bathroom sink every night so we could take a bath. This ritual soon became a treasured time for us to spend together. The memories of that day came flooding back as I bathed you; they were so clear and so moving that it felt like they had happened yesterday. I remember the way your small hand reached out to grab my finger as you looked up at me, your eyes glimmering with delight and purity. My heart melted at that same instant, which confirmed how deeply I loved you, my dear baby.

You could only fall asleep at night when you were cuddled up against my chest, and your gentle breaths mingled with mine in the still darkness. I would cling to you, feeling the steady beat of your heart against mine as if it were a lullaby that would soothe my restless spirit. I was taken back to a period before you were born when I would rock you softly in my stomach while sitting in the rocking rocker your dad had brought home for me during those times as I sang and read to you.

Even then, while I was rubbing my stomach and giving you comforting, loving whispers, I knew that you would always be my greatest happiness and my constant companion on this journey we call parenting. And while I sang to you the lovely melodies of Bible hymns, full of promise and hope, I experienced a wave of calm, knowing that no matter where life led us, we would always have one other.

There, in Baton Rouge, I would frequently find myself strolling down to the Piggy Wiggly supermarket. I started making the trip to the grocery store with you along as a regular routine after the shelter. During those times, my WIC card was a lifeline since it allowed me to buy the necessary formula. I occasionally had to turn to begging when the shelter's supplies ran low because I had no money left over for food for myself. It was a humble experience, but my first concern was making sure all the kids, you especially, had enough to eat.

Even with the difficulties, I was committed to taking care of you. I saw to it that you had a warm bed every night, food in your belly, and clothes on your back. I would never consider my wants before seeing to it that yours were satisfied. My only concern was for you, and I based every choice I made on ensuring your well-being.

I would frequently take a stroll to the nearby Baton Rouge library to escape the monotony of living in a shelter. I traveled there almost daily, overcoming whatever barriers I encountered in order to temporarily leave the shelter. The library turned into a haven where I could temporarily forget about our problems and lose myself in a different world. No matter how big or little the undertaking, you were always at my side.

Not only was walking to the library a means of getting out of the shelter, but it was also a way for us to establish regularity and normalcy. It provided us with a motivation to get outside, take in the clean air, and discover the world beyond our current problems.

The calm nooks and book rows of the library offered a tranquil break from the turmoil and uncertainty that pervaded our surroundings.

I made sure you were with me at all times throughout it all. You were always in my arms or by my side, whether we were strolling to the library or the grocery store.

You were such a sweet baby, happy to play and sleep through the chaos, which brought me some calm. I could always count on you to be cheerful and serene during those trying times. I waited impatiently for a break, spending endless hours on the web seeking jobs while you played or slept soundly. But no matter how hard I tried, I had no luck at all. The process felt much more difficult as a result of the depressing lack of responses.

For me, it was particularly difficult because I had no formal schooling. Your dad was often reminding me of this and hanging it over my head. He never missed an occasion. He would tell me I would never be as smart as the other women he compared me to and call me stupid for not finishing school. His remarks were like knives, piercing my self-worth and strengthening my fears.

I used to wonder why he thought we should be married in the first place. He was aware right away that I lacked a degree and a bright future. Despite being fully aware of these realities, he nevertheless made the decision to marry me. This gave me the constant feeling that I was being utilized for strange purposes. My sense of uncertainty and hurt was only exacerbated by the lack of answers and the ongoing denigration.

Trapped in the car, a vehicle that represents both freedom and imprisonment, I felt completely abandoned in my unemployed state. I felt like life was a burden, weighing me down with its incessant trials. But in the middle of all of this, there was one unwavering promise: to make sure you showed up on time for each and every doctor's appointment. It turned into a delicate dance, where dates were rescheduled with extreme care to avoid your father's impending meddling.

Amid all of this chaos, the shelter offered a lifeline—a driver assigned to transport us to and from doctor's appointments. I started these adventures with you, clinging to this lifeline that provided hope in the face of uncertainty. However, in the midst of these unrelenting difficulties, heartbreaking news about your fragile state arrived. After birth, your entry into the world was so unstable that your fragile leg became twisted. What is the outcome? A heavy brace, like a confining shell around your leg. Despite this setback, I continued to go with you to all of your appointments, remaining a silent observer of your struggles and victories.

Then, as we sat in the sterile confines of the doctor's office one fateful day, a ray of hope appeared in our path. The doctor took off the brace with deft hands, revealing the amazing transformation underneath. Adversity had twisted your leg, but now it stood true and straight, freed from the bonds of its former prison of the brace. We did it together, sweetie! We fought through everything and came out stronger than ever.

Chapter 7

Your dad eventually found out where we were staying one day. My heart was thumping with worry and terror at the time, as I can well recall. He was getting close to where we were hiding, attempting to stay out of his grasp. Thank goodness, my caseworker at the shelter was just as determined to keep us safe as I was to protect you. She was aware of how serious things were and how dangerous we were.

For women like myself who had fled violent homes, the shelter where we were sheltering served as a temporary haven. Despite its tiny size, the facility provided us with a sense of safety and belonging. The employees were kind and committed, always willing to go above and beyond to help those in need.

During this difficult period, my caseworker in particular was a ray of hope for me. She was knowledgeable and compassionate, and she recognized that I was going through emotional and psychological distress in addition to the physical risk we were facing.

I experienced a panic attack when the cops arrived at the shelter. They were talking about taking you away from me, and I could hear them. It hurt to think about losing you. It was terrible to think that they could simply take you away after I had worked so hard to keep you secure. My caseworker took immediate action. Her resourcefulness and fast thinking came in very handy at this very crucial moment.

To give us some time, she chose to conceal us in a motel, sufficiently removed from the shelter. The motel was a modest, unremarkable location outside of town. Although it was by no means opulent, it gave us the much-needed privacy. Even though we were only there for a few days, they were some of the longest days of my life. My pulse raced with panic at the sound of every sound, every knock on the door. I was scared your dad would find us and take you away, so I was always looking over my shoulder.

And then they discovered us. I still recall the same moment I received court documents. Upon seeing those documents, my knees gave way. I experienced a sense of having the earth lifted off of me. The realization that I didn't have an attorney and that my family didn't have the funds to pay one caused me to cry. It was devastating to think that your dad, who could afford to employ a first-rate lawyer, would take you away. I was aware that his father would do whatever it took to get you away from me.

According to the court documents, I'm not qualified to take care of you. They brought up my postpartum depression, which is common among new moms but frequently misinterpreted. They portrayed me as unstable and unfit to raise my own child by using it as a weapon against me.

They also brought up the fact that I had fled with you following a difficult circumstance with your dad, turning my frantic desire to shield you into something negative.

My thoughts and feelings were racing through my head. It was getting harder and harder to keep focused. I had the impression that I was submerged in a sea of anxiety and doubt. However, my caseworker came to my aid once more in the midst of this confusion. She was able to locate a lawyer to represent me in court. This lawyer was familiar with the intricacies of situations similar to me and has ties to the Baton Rouge women's shelter.

Gonzales, Louisiana, was the planned location of the court proceeding. The closer the day got, the more anxious I became. I was aware that our future could be decided by this hearing. It was intimidating to think about being in front of a judge, up against your dad and his formidable legal team.

The most difficult aspect was having the guts to tell the lawyer all that had been going on. Despite the daunting experience, I managed to complete it. The lawyer took his time listening to me describe the entire experience. He made sure I was ready for the big day in court by being very thorough and meticulous. I was nervous, but his advice gave me a little peace of mind.

My grandmother and her friend came down to support me in court on the day of the hearing. Their presence served as a reassuring reminder that I wasn't fighting this battle alone. I recall feeling more anxious than ever as I entered that courtroom. My level of anxiety was almost terrible, and I prayed a lot in the hopes that God would sustain me during it all. The agonizing wait went on, with every minute seeming like an eternity as we waited anxiously for our turn.

At last, we received a call. Then the judge summoned the two lawyers to his chambers. We were only permitted to bring our attorneys back there, not your dad or me, for whatever reason. They were in there for what felt like an eternity. My worry increased with every second that went by. I noticed the delighted look on your dad's lawyer's face when they eventually came out. Full of confidence, he came over to your dad, and I heard him tell him they had won.

She gave you to me when I got there, her eyes saddened. I had lost the fight to keep you, and the most heartbreaking moment of my life was holding you in my arms.

I found it incomprehensible that the judge had granted your dad sole custody. I knew deep down that you had an amazing mother in me. My love for you had remained unwavering despite the turbulent circumstances and my postpartum depression. I had battled valiantly to safeguard you and create a secure and nurturing atmosphere, but the Gonzales, Louisiana, court had let me down.

We were let down by the system, and I had no choice but to give you to your dad. My sense of powerlessness was terrible. Even though I was sorry to see you go, the court's ruling was definitive. Even if every cell in my body cried out against it, I had to obey. My world seemed to have collapsed, and I could not stand the anguish of losing you to him.

I only had an hour with you before I had to say goodbye. Even though those sixty minutes didn't seem long, they were the most important ones in my life. The timer appeared to be running faster, taking away valuable moments with you every second. The setting, a restaurant where we were meeting your dad's parents, seemed anything but neutral to me. They kept a close eye on me the entire time, examining every move I made with you. I needed to be watched over because it was so dysfunctional, as if my love for you required observation or interrogation. I treasured every day I had with you so much, and I will always remember them with vivid clarity.

I tried to memorize every detail of your little face while I was holding you in my arms. Everything about you was perfect, even your innocent eyes and your soft skin. In those last moments, I tried to express all the love I had for you by holding you so tightly and whispering my final "I love yous." But eventually it was time to go, and they instructed me to give you over. Their statements broke my heart. I resisted with every fiber of my being to let you go. As your dad's father took you out of my arms and gently placed you in your baby carrier, I sobbed uncontrollably.

Even though you were too young to comprehend what was happening—you were only three months old—your cries mirrored my own suffering.

The moment they drove away, I broke completely; I couldn't handle the overwhelming sorrow and loss that engulfed me; my body shook with uncontrollable sobs, and my mind spiraled into a state of madness. I heard your cries, and each sob felt like a dagger in my heart. That was the last time I would ever see you again as a child. I stood there, frozen in anguish, watching the car disappear from sight, taking you further away from me with each passing second

I felt as though a piece of myself had been torn away, leaving an empty space, and the pain was too much to handle. My world was forever altered by the pain of losing you after that day.

I eventually moved back to Texas after you were handed over to your dad by the court. I had no reason to stay where I was now that you were gone. I needed to figure out how to fill the void in my life. I had to get back on my feet, which meant obtaining some stability, getting a car, and getting a job. I was aware that without my family's help, I could not handle any of this. They were my compass and the only people who could get me through this difficult period. Upon my eventual return home, though, I was overcome by a feeling of inertia. I was unable to motivate myself to do anything for a very long time. Depression was suffocating. I plunged into a dark abyss, tormented by intense nightmares and fits of irrational rage.

My coping strategies were harmful. I started drinking a lot in an attempt to block out the memories and the pain. I became restless and my nights would often last into the wee hours of the morning as I made a valiant effort to get away from my thoughts. I messaged your dad when I was more coherent, hoping he would at least send me some photos or at least a conversation about you. At first, he did, and I got a little glimpse into your life for a short while. However, that window closed quickly. He eventually stopped replying and blocked me entirely, along with his family. They knew that by severing our relationship, they could get me out of the picture, which is what they wanted.

I had never felt more hopeless and depressed than I did after experiencing such an unbearable loss. I even made another attempt at suicide during my darkest hours because I didn't think there would be any other way without you. I didn't have the strength to handle your absence. My family and friends' unwavering support was the only thing that gave me the willpower to carry on. They came together for me, giving me the emotional support I needed to begin putting my life back together. I also started going to a counselor. This expert assistance proved to be a vital component of my recovery journey, providing me with the skills and techniques I needed to control my grief and start thinking about the future.

It was, and still is, very difficult! No matter how much time goes by, the suffering and struggles of those days seem to never go away. As the years passed, I noticed that my strength was decreasing and that my resolve was being eroded a little bit each time. Despite this difficulty, life went on. In the midst of the mayhem, I began to discover a tiny bit of normalcy. I came into the life of a gentle and understanding man, and the two of us became parents to another gorgeous baby girl. This new chapter gave me a fresh sense of direction, but I never gave up on the dream that we would one day be reunited in God's perfect timing. You are and always will be an enduring fixture in my heart, deserving of infinite love. Even though she has never met you, your half-sister will grow up understanding the full extent of your significance to us and your life story.

I have poured my heart into letters to you every night since I lost you. Composing these letters has been my savior; it's how we can maintain our relationship strong and alive. I feel like I'm talking to you directly through my words, keeping that close bond we had. It feels almost like I'm holding you in my arms once more, reading to you and whispering stories to you the way I always would have. The days keep coming, unrelenting and uncaring, but my love for you is constant, sincere, and pure. Neither my memories of you nor the tales I tell the world will ever fade. To make sure you are never forgotten, your legacy will be preserved, honored, and celebrated.

How precious you are to me is only known by God. I can't wait to see my baby girl again; he has been getting me ready for that day. I want to give you so much to experience and so much to share with you. I have been reserving things for you ever since your dad won the case against me in court. It has been heartbreaking to watch each year pass without being able to call your dad to visit or talk to you. He cut me off from communicating with you in any way, but I wasn't going to let that stop me. I have a ton of birthday cards as well as holiday cards for Christmas, Easter, Valentine's Day, Halloween, and Thanksgiving saved. I've kept other treasures as well, but above all, I've kept the letters I write to you. I keep writing them, giving each word my whole being.

I wish I could have witnessed your first crawl, first set of steps, and first spoken words. I never got to experience all those priceless moments because of your dad. Though sad, the fact remains. Even though I've never heard your voice, I'm sure it's beautiful. I am confident that despite everything, you are developing into a stunning young woman. After so many years apart, I hope to see you again and embrace you in my arms.

I've had countless visions of our reunion. I picture us sitting down and going through everything I've kept for you. Every letter and card I send you is proof of my affection and desire for you. I've kept souvenirs from special occasions and holidays in the hopes that you would feel the love I've always had for you, even though I'm far away.

My thoughts and life experiences are captured in every letter I've written to you. They are full of my dreams for you, advice, and stories. I've expressed in writing how much I wanted to be there for you and how much I missed you. Despite not being able to see it with my own eyes, I have conveyed my pride in the person you are growing into and my hopes for the future.

The hurt of not reaching your goals has been unbearable. I wanted to be there to support you at your first game or recital, as well as on your first day of school. I wanted to be a part of your daily life, to help you with your homework, and to tuck you in at night.

Even though your dad's choice to keep us apart has hurt me greatly, it hasn't lessened my love for you. You have a bright future ahead of you, and I have no doubt that we will cross paths again. I'm holding out hope that you'll find me and we can catch up on our missed time. I will continue to write, save mementos, and love you from a distance until that time.

Chapter 8

oodbyes are never easy. The toughest part, I've found, isn't the initial sting of loss, the sharp, debilitating ache that takes your breath away. It's the slow, persistent thrum in your chest, the constant reminder of a space left empty. It's trying to move forward with a broken heart, each step weighed down by a sorrow that feels as heavy as the world.

There are moments, fleeting and bright, where a semblance of happiness returns. A genuine laugh escapes my lips, a sunny day lifts my spirits, and for a stolen breath, I forget the hollowness that resides within. But then, like a tide pulling back, the reality washes over me again. You're not here. This joy, however real it feels in the moment, is incomplete without you to share it with.

Your sister, though, has become a lifeline. Her presence in my life is a wellspring of unexpected joy, a ray of sunshine that pierces through the fog of grief. Seeing your reflection in her smile, hearing your echoes in her laughter, fills me with a warmth I didn't think possible again. It's a bittersweet comfort, a reminder of what I've lost intertwined with the gratitude for what remains.

And writing to you, of course. I can sort through the unrestrained emotions churning inside of me when I try putting pen to the paper or as soon as my fingertips touch the keyboard. There's a strange comfort in expressing myself and reaching out to you even if you're a great distance away. It serves as a bridge to span the gap separating us and a means of keeping you close.

It is incredibly healing to read about other people's experiences with grief and their frankness and sensitivity. It serves as a reminder that I'm not the only one going through this; that this broken sensation and the need for what's missing are common human experiences. I feel a sense of camaraderie and connection with those who share my grief because of what they have said.

Despite the physical distance between us, I can feel your presence at these times of connection and shared experience. There's a gentle solace in it, a whisper in the breeze, a reminder that our love knows no bounds to time or place. There's a glimmer of optimism that, eventually, my heart's torn pieces will mend, and my happiness will be whole again.

God is good, and he will reunite us back together in his time. This is a truth I hold close to my heart, a beacon in the storm of missing you both. My path to healing is filled with priceless memories of your warmth and smiles; healing is a journey, not a destination. Even in your absence, the brightness you brought into my life, my little daughter, never goes out. The bond we share transcends distance, a connection woven from love and understanding. And to my precious other daughter, you too hold a special place in my heart. Together, you are my world, the very air I breathe.

The memory of that letter, the one where I poured out my heart about forgiving your father, brings a bittersweet comfort. It wasn't easy, that act of letting go. The hurt he caused ran deep, a wound that festered for far too long. But anger, I came to realize, was a heavy burden to carry. It weighed me down, clouding the love I hold for all of you. So, with a strength I never knew I possessed, I chose forgiveness.

Releasing the bonds of bitterness that tied me is the goal of forgiveness, not endorsing his behavior. It's about realizing that he might be the guy he is now because of his own wounds. While it doesn't make the hurt go away, it does let me move on with a lighter heart. Maybe in the far future, he will also experience healing. Perhaps he'll be happy with someone else.

I cling to these priceless memories until then. I hear your laughter over the sound of rustling leaves, and I see your smiles in the early morning light. I am not separate from you; you are a part of who I am.

The way things turn out is hilarious. Reuniting with your dad following the chaos of the wedding? Big mistake, everybody said. I felt lost, humiliated and heartbroken. But as things often happen, life had other ideas. I rebuilt my life gradually, perhaps with a hint of forgiveness and a glimmer of optimism hanging on. We then crossed paths once more. A deliberate reconnecting rather than a dramatic reunion. A spark rekindled between two injured people. You then arrived. The most beautiful surprise there is. Yes, there were doubts and "what if?" moments that crossed my mind. But the love I feel for you now is beyond anything I've ever experienced. That terrible day, in hindsight, seems like a disaster. But it led me here, to you, and that's all that matters. Maybe things really do work themselves out, even when you least expect it.

That's why, when you grow up, I want you to take your time finding the right partner. Someone who cherishes you, makes you feel cherished, someone who sees you as the most important part of their life, just like you are to mine. You deserve every wonderful thing life has to offer, every dream you chase. And never, ever forget, no matter what life throws your way – happy, sad, or anything in between – my arms are always open. No matter how busy I may seem, there's nothing more important than you.

I can hardly wait to see my beautiful daughter again, to hold you close and witness all the amazing things you'll accomplish. Imagining you on your wedding day, me helping you fix your dress, a tear in my eye as I watch you embark on your own adventure of love and motherhood – it fills my heart with so much joy. Remember, darling, no matter where life takes you, I'll always be here, waiting with open arms, your biggest cheerleader, your rock.

Every night, I look for a shining star, its light a beacon in the inky expanse. It's during these quiet moments, bathed in the soft glow, that my deepest wish takes flight. I close my eyes and picture the day you'll finally call me "Mom." The sound of that single word, tripping off your tiny tongue, would be a melody unlike any other. It would be a symphony of pure, unadulterated joy, washing away the ache in my heart.

Then, another wish surfaces, just as potent – to hear you whisper "I love you" with that innocent trust that only children possess. The very thought melts my insides, a warm gooey mess of pure, maternal love. I imagine wrapping you in my arms, the feeling of your small body nestled against mine, a silent promise of forever etched in that embrace.

Knowing I'm not alone in this yearning brings a strange sort of comfort. There are countless parents out there, hearts echoing with the same emptiness, the same yearning. For them, too, I send up a silent prayer, a plea for solace in this difficult time. Don't lose hope; I want to scream at the vast, indifferent sky. Don't let misery dim the light in your eyes. Because, as the popular saying states, what goes

around comes around. Karma, fate, the universe –
whatever you choose to name it – has a way of
balancing things out.

Be happy, my love, and always remember how
much I do love you! This letter isn't just for you, but
for every child separated from their parents, every
parent yearning for their child's embrace. To the
mothers and fathers across the globe – perhaps you
lost a child through a heartbreaking court battle, the
intervention of CPS, a cruel twist of fate, or the
agonizing uncertainty of them being missing.
Whatever the reason, please don't let despair cloud
your heart. Don't let sorrow extinguish the light of
hope. Hold onto your faith, for even in the darkest
night, God's love remains a constant beacon.

I am aware that the pain can be unbearable, a
constant burden on the soul. But please, try not to let
your pain control you. Have faith that better times are
coming, like sunshine peeking through gloomy
clouds. Have faith in God's plan despite your
inability to understand it. Give your troubles to Him,

trusting that He can restore even the most broken hearts.

Written in a whisper on the wind of hope, this letter serves as a prayer. I hope it makes its way to the people who most need it, providing comfort in the face of sorrow and the willpower to go on. Have trust that even the most difficult aspirations can come true if you have steadfast faith. You are not alone. God's love surrounds you, and with it, the promise of comfort and joy, waiting to bloom anew.

"Those we love and lose are always connected by heartstrings into infinity." –

Terri Guillemets

Made in the USA
Middletown, DE
14 October 2024

62659925R00073